KEN WARD

Discovering
Backpacking

D1337755

SHIRE PUBLICATIONS LTD

Contents

Set in 9 point Times by Oxford Publishing Services and printed in Great Britain by C.I. Thomas & Sons (Haverfordwest) Ltd, Press Buildings, Merlin's Bridge, Haverfordwest.

1. Introduction

Take a tent, a sleeping bag, some food and a map and disappear into the hills to wander at will. That, very simply, is backpacking.

Living in a community produces pressures on the individual. The more independent the individual the greater the pressures. And those pressures appear to increase proportionally with the size of the community and the degree of importance it attaches to materialistic acquisitions.

Backpacking is an escape to independence.

The laws

But real independence does not mean lack of responsibility. Indeed, if you are to survive a backpacking adventure, and if you are to return to the community fitter in both mind and body, then there are laws to be observed. These laws, which you will largely discover and formulate yourself, form the unwritten rules of successful backpacking.

This book aims to shorten the learning period and to show that anyone can learn to escape into the freedom of the countryside.

Backpacking is open to anyone who can walk. Age is not important. You are old enough when your sense of responsibility says you are. And at the other end of the time scale, you are too old when that same sense of responsibility gently suggests it is so. It is true that the young tigers will go striding over the hilltops seeking out the most arduous routes in the most demanding conditions, whilst others will discover their freedom along gentle valleys and kindly lowlands. Sex is no decider, although the majority of backpackers are men.

The season for backpacking covers twelve months of every year. Certainly in the British Isles there is very little difference in the weather over that period. Temperatures are lower in the winter but many a June day has found me digging into my pack, on some windswept slope, for the gloves not wanted on a December day. Part of the skill is learning to equip yourself for every type of terrain in any set of conditions. Anyone equipping himself just to enjoy those balmy days that occasionally break upon us in the summer is doomed to disaster. By the same law, on a winter expedition it is sensible to have with you a light shirt, lip salve and those tinted snow goggles which suddenly become sunglasses.

Some backpackers are satisfied just to exist, to walk, to fill lungs with fresh air and to experience the visual pleasures of the great outdoors. For others it is a great opportunity to study bird and animal life under ideal conditions, or to develop an interest in plant life, geology, archaeology or any other study that benefits from the freedom to move in any direction, at any pace. For some it is an opportunity to study themselves, with a minimum of external influences.

Discovering the countryside

Backpacking is the ideal way to discover Britain. Only the walker can truly appreciate the subtleties of its geography. The backdrop of a range of hills seen from a highway could as easily be painted as a mural on the side of a factory. A hill is the sounds of a hill, the smell and feel of a hill. The motorist knows nothing of it. The car park with a viewpoint down the gorge is a fraud. The real view is on the cliff edge, a quarter of a mile round the bend, where it is impractical for the car to go. The motorist sees the picture that it has been decided he will see, and it is identical to that seen by car-trapped millions.

He travels in fixed lines determined by others, in a capsule in which he attempts to re-create in miniature his usual environment, with comfortable seats, music and heater. He could be travelling in a three-dimensional television set, seeing the programme, without becoming part of it.

Only the walker is privileged to discover nature. The real dwellers of the countryside have been driven from the highway areas by noise and poison. To find them you must wander into their territory on their terms.

The cyclist comes nearer than the motorist to knowing what the countryside really offers but he too is very largely obliged to stick to the narrow strips set aside for the motorcar.

Hikers, walkers, ramblers, or whatever name is in vogue, have always known this. But the backpacker has an advantage even over them. For the backpacker carries with him his shelter and his food. The rambler, whatever he discovers or whatever befalls, must very largely stick to a fixed programme finding accommodation or transport before nightfall. The backpacker goes when he likes and stops when he likes. If the weather turns sour, or he is tired, or he just feels like stopping, the backpacker pitches his tent, makes a meal and rolls out his sleeping bag. And only he and the map know where he is.

The rewards

The rewards of backpacking are many. For one thing you will see much that is wonderful. You will probably remember breathtaking sunrises seen from lofty platforms in the Scottish highlands. You may be lucky enough to compare the dramatic sight and sound of a waterfall with the soft rhythmic lapping and shimmering light on a large lake, and you will certainly see more of the British Isles than you thought possible.

You will also be fitter, not just because you use muscles again which you have had no cause to employ for a long time; not because you have gently pumped away the fat forming around a willing heart; and not because you are now filling lungs to maximum capacity with air so clean that you can smell the sweetness. But you will find that you learn to care for your body as the proud workman cares for his tools. You will remember that your body is your most useful item of kit and you will get it running smoother than it has done for years.

You will make many friends. Backpackers, although rarely gregarious, delight in discussing items of equipment, routes and pitches. With some it will be just a nod on the path, whilst with others it will be a pitch shared or an evening spent together in a little pub miles away from the main centres of population. I do not recall ever meeting a backpacker out on a fell who has not replied to my greeting with a grin.

But the real reward comes at the end of the trek, when it is all over. It is a feeling that grows as the aches in your bones disappear and as tiredness is slept away. It is the deep and satisfying sense of achievement. If this book results in you experiencing that, just once, then it will have achieved its aim.

2. The weight of your pack

I once walked with a backpacker for a whole day on the Pennine Way. In the evening he pitched his camp a little further on than I did and I never saw him again, but I remember he proposed a theory regarding carrying unnecessary items of kit. He maintained that packing a comb was equal to lifting thirty-two common building bricks. His proposal was that if you took a comb that weighed, for instance, half an ounce (14 grams), and you tucked this into the top of your right boot, then every time you lifted your right foot you would lift an extra half an ounce. He then suggested that if you walked a mile with the offending comb, you would probably take eighteen hundred paces, which means that you would lift the comb nine hundred times. If, however, you did a modest trek of eight miles then you would probably take 14,400 paces, which would mean you would raise your now weary right foot 7,200 times. He assured me that 7,200 times half an ounce (14 grams) was 222 pounds (100 kg), which is also the approximate weight of thirty-two common building bricks!

I am sure that he knew there was a flaw somewhere in this theory and that is probably why I was unable to catch him next day, to question him further. However, his point was made.

It is generally agreed that a maximum pack weight is equal to one third of your body weight, so that an 11 stone (69 kg) backpacker's maximum should be not more than 50 pounds (23 kg). Without doubt the most difficult obstacle the novice has to overcome is learning how to keep a pack weight down to an acceptable level.

Consider the following imaginary equipment list:

	pounds	ounces	grams
Carrying sack	5	0	2268
See Chapter 4.			
Tent	5	0	2268
See Chapter 6.			
Insulated sleeping pad	1	4	567
See Chapter 7.			
Sleeping bag	5	0	2268
See Chapter 7.			
Water bottle, with 1½ pints (0.85 litres) of water	2	0	907
Empty 3 ounces (85 grams).			
Water carrier	0	4	113
See Chapter 8.			
Mug	0	2	57

Plastic, half pint (0.28 litres) capacity. Clip

	pounds	ounces	grams
rather than conventional handle enables you to clip to belt or side of pan when ground is uneven. Keep lightweight tea-spoon clipped to mug by elastic band, always ready for brew-up or adding lemonade crystals to water.			
Matches, three boxes	0	1	28
Stow in different parts of pack, all plastic wrapped. In spares kit also carry a few windproof matches (see below).			
Stove	2	0	907
Fuel	2	0	907
Butane S200 Gaz. Full cylinder weighs 10 ounces (284 grams) and will burn for about 2 hours 40 minutes. Boils 1 pint (0.57 litres) of water in 12 minutes. One cylinder will give you about thirty-six half-pint (0.28 litre) mugs of tea or instant soup.			
Tranqia meths stove has a capacity of about one eighth of a pint (0.07 litres), which will burn for about 20 minutes and will boil half a pint (0.28 litres) of water in about 3 minutes. (It will burn for 1 hour with simmer ring down and boil half a pint (0.28 litres) in 9 minutes.) In practice 1 pint (0.57 litres) of meths will make about fifty half-pint (0.28 litre) mugs of tea or soup depending on how efficiently you conserve the heat.			
Windshield	0	3	85
See Chapter 8.			
Cooking pans, plate, cutlery	0	12	340
See Chapter 8.			
Pan gripper	0	2	57
See Chapter 8.			
Washing-up kit	0	1	28
A Jiffy cloth sheds grease and dries easily. A useful pan scrubber is a block of foam rubber with a scourer backing.			
Personal washing kit	0	8	227
Hotel-size soap, 1 ounce (28 grams). Small toothpaste tube or salt. Traveller's toothbrush. Shaving cream repacked into 2 ounce (14 gram) container. Dis-			

	pounds	ounces	grams
posable razor. Steel mirror. Small face flannel. Antiseptic wipes in foil sachets make good substitute for aftershave to make you feel civilised.			
Small towel	0	6	*170*
A baby's nappy is ideal but get it dyed a dark colour first in order not to offend you after a few days.			
First-aid kit	0	9	*255*
See Chapter 10.			
Torch	0	9	*255*
See Chapter 10.			
Maps	0	8	*227*
Buy them flat; they are less weight.			
Compass and whistle	0	2	*57*
See Chapter 10.			
Stearin candle	0	5	*142*
A long-life candle will give you adequate illumination to cook and read by and help generate warmth in the tent. Stand in a flat pan with a piece of foil behind to stop flickering and give you most of the light.			
Kit of spares	0	4	*113*
It is a good idea to equip yourself with an odd-job bag, but keep the weight down. In this you can keep a spare boot lace, a length of nylon cord, a tiny roll of water- proof adhesive tape, safety pins, two small plastic clothes pegs, nightlight, windproof matches, small polythene bags, two giant paper clips, folding tin opener on cord (less than 1 ounce, 28.35 grams) and a handful of elastic bands.			
Paper handkerchiefs, toilet paper	0	1	*28*
Keep in plastic bag in your back pocket _ you never know!			
Handkerchiefs	0	2	*57*
Khaki or dark blue are the most sensible colours.			
Woollen shirt	1	2	*510*
Should button right down the front, have long sleeves and a tail long enough to cover all of your trunk.			
Woollen pullover	1	7	*652*

	pounds	ounces	grams
Marks and Spencer will provide you with a fine, zip-fronted cardigan with pockets at a very good price. See Chapter 5.			
Underwear	0	4	*113*
Cotton is better than man-made fibres.			
Small socks	0	2	*57*
Spare pair.			
Long socks	0	7	*198*
Spare pair.			
Woollen hat or balaclava helmet	0	4	*113*
Useful when the wind gets cold and indispensable to stop the great heat loss through the head when you are tucked up in your sleeping bag. See Chapter 7.			
Gloves	0	2	*57*
Woollen pair usually suffices. For really cold-weather walking you could invest in nylon, fur-lined gloves, 8 ounces (226.8 grams). See Chapter 5.			
Waterproof jacket	1	6	*624*
See Chapter 5.			
Overtrousers	0	10	*284*
See Chapter 5.			
Light gym shoes	1	10	*737*
Welcome change from boots about camp. Very useful to slip on outside a pub that insists 'No boots'.			
Polar suit	2	0	*907*
Ideal for sleeping and about-camp wear. Zip-fronted jacket could well replace the woollen jacket listed above. See Chapter 5.			
Boot dubbin	0	1	*28*
Apply it with your fingers. See Chapter 3.			
Snow goggles	0	2	*57*
Useful in driving rain and snow, high winds or bright sunlight in snow conditions.			
Snacks	1	0	*454*
A few snacks easy to hand are useful to help find that extra energy during the day, or when morale is flagging. Mars bar, 1.8 ounces (51 grams).			

	pounds	*ounces*	*grams*
Bar chocolate, 1.8 ounces (51 grams). Dextrose sweets, 2 ounces (57 grams). Callard and Bowser butterscotch, 3.5 ounces (99 grams).			
Tea kit	1	2	*510*
Forty tea bags, 6 ounces (170 grams). Ten coffee sachets, 1 ounce (28 grams). Forty wrapped sugar lumps (two), 4 ounces (113 grams). Tube of Nestles condensed milk, 7 ounces (198 grams) (equal to five eighths of a pint, 0.35 litres, of milk with sugar added).			
Light haversack	0	6	*170*
Folds up into tiny pouch. Use as kit bag for dry clothes. Ideal for use when visiting shops or for day expedition from base camp.			
Total	39	7	*17,802*

To this must be added the weight of food, which will always weigh at least 1½ pounds (680 grams) a day, as we will discover in Chapter 8. The nice thing about food is that you gradually eat your way through it so that at the end of a ten-day expedition your pack is at least 15 pounds (6.8 kilograms) lighter and you positively float along.

For winter trekking you will probably want to include a duvet jacket (2 pounds, 907 grams), and if you plan to do high-level walking in snow and ice you may also want to have an ice-axe (2 pounds, 907 grams) with you and perhaps crampons (2 pounds, 907 grams).

The equipment list above is not necessarily the ideal list but is included to demonstrate how easily weight builds up. The utility of every article must be considered and you must be quite ruthless. You will reluctantly omit some favourite items which theoretically should be invaluable. That Swiss army knife, for instance, with a tool for every conceivable situation, including getting Boy Scouts out of horses' hooves, weighs 6 ounces (170 grams).

Your 'fingerprint' kit

Equip yourself with a small pocket balance and take it with you when you go shopping. Outdoor equipment shops are quite used to backpackers who weigh every item when considering a purchase.

Carefully work at your kit list until you believe you have it honed down to a high level of efficiency, with a carrying weight which will allow you to enjoy your trek. Only you can compile this list. You will, undoubtedly, make many changes as a result of experience gained in different weather conditions or terrains. But it will always be your own compilation, reflecting your preferences, hobbies or interests. And it will be as unique as your fingerprint.

In time, especially after a trek of several days, this monster on your back will become as much a part of you as the turtle's shell is part of the turtle, and you will become almost affectionately disposed towards it. For with you is everything you may need to meet any situation, and awareness of that is very satisfying. If the weather turns hot, you can dress for it. If the elements turn savagely against you, there is every protection you need, including shelter and a warm bed. Cut a finger, you can dress it. Tear a garment, you can mend it. Feel hungry and you can take a snack or a three-course meal. Feel tired and you can sit down where you are and brew a cup of tea. It is a completeness that money cannot buy back in the urban hubbub. Many times when waiting at an airport, travelling on business or even shopping I have longed for the comfort to be derived from that 40 pound (18 kilogram) life support system.

So choose carefully and shoulder the load cheerfully. You will share many adventures together.

3. Boots and foot care

No matter how perfect your kit collection, or how precise your navigation, or how good you become with a stove, or even how fit you are, successful backpacking depends on just two things – your feet.

Backpacking is many things to different people, but for everyone it is walking. And this requires good strong leg muscles and, most of all, good-natured healthy feet.

Feet to the backpacker are like wheels to the motorist. If anything happens to either of them, then movement ceases. But the motorist, of course, carries a spare!

So let us consider these feet. They are your travel ticket to the hills. It will pay you to treat them well and pamper them a little. Bathe them often and keep toenails cut short and straight across. And let them see the sun from time to time.

Exercise them by steadying yourself against a chair and raise yourself on to your toes, then rock back on your heels. Do you still have control of your toes? Can you pick up a button with them?

Some backpackers believe in hardening the skin by bathing their feet in alcohol, but exposure to the air and sun is all they need. Do not keep them hidden like white roots under a stone.

Take with you on a trek about 2 ounces (57 grams) of Vaseline Intensive Care (sold by most chemists). When you know a day is likely to put heavy demands on them, rub a little in thoroughly, all over the feet and up the ankles. This will help to prevent those hot spots which become blisters.

When walking, be constantly aware of the development of hot spots. At the very first hint of discomfort, wherever you are, stop and take off your boot. It may be caused by a tiny piece of grit that escaped your early morning foot inspection or it may be a crease in your sock. Apply a piece of adhesive plaster, whatever the cause, and you may well avoid a blister. If a blister does develop then cover with a piece of foam-backed Moleskin, Dr Scholl's gift to backpackers. Do not be afraid to put on plasters. It is better to have a foot looking like an Egyptian mummy than the awful discomfort of walking on painful feet. Be wary of bursting blisters with the famous sterilised needle. Most blisters disappear after twenty-four hours and the risk of infection is best avoided.

When in camp never go about barefoot, not even for a few paces. The chance of your stepping on a piece of glass or rusty tin is remote, but the possible damage makes this risk unacceptable.

Your socks should be carefully chosen, so that they are neither too big nor too small, and always woollen. Wool absorbs moisture, while man-made fibres will cause your feet to overheat and swell. Smooth on your socks carefully. They should have no lumps or darns. It is sensible to wear two pairs of socks. Apart from the extra padding this gives, they also absorb friction between boot and foot.

Choosing your boots

Always walk in boots. Some walkers declare that they are happier in shoes, but take my advice and train your feet to walk in boots. Boots usually have a broader sole in order best to spread the weight, and the high collar gives support to lessen the chances of a twisted ankle. A boot can also take a thicker sole to prevent you feeling through them every stone on the path.

Your boots will be of leather. Choose walking boots, not climbing boots. Climbing boots are often unnecessarily heavy and incorporate metal sole stiffeners, which are too rigid for the walker. Vibram or Kletter soles are moulded after the fashion of the old alpinist's stud patterns and they will give good wear and a good grip. However, on hard snow, ice, steep wet grass or mossy rocks the adhesion can suddenly disappear and care is needed.

On no account accept inexpensive so called 'fell boots' produced from canvas-backed cheap suede with soles moulded from doubtful materials. I was once leading a trek to Everest Base Camp and was horrified to find that one of the party was wearing such boots. They exploded on the third day.

Buy your boots from a shop that has a good reputation and a wide stock and be prepared to listen to their advice. Take with you an extra pair of socks and put these on before fitting the boots. Your feet should not feel compressed. Remember that a hard working foot will swell and if the woollen socks are too compressed then they will lose their insulation and you will have cold feet or even, in very cold conditions, risk frostnip and frostbite. Stub your foot well down into the boot so that your toes can just touch the inside of the toe cap. If they do more than just reach, then you will have painful toes in long descents. You should also be able to push your finger down between the back of your foot and the stiffener. Lace up the boot, not too tightly, and walk about the shop, up and down steps if possible. Your heel should rise no more than about one eighth of an inch (3 millimetres) inside the boot when walking. If it rises any more, you will develop blisters or a painful Achilles tendon. This is the most important purchase of your backpacking equipment so take your time. Some specialist shops will agree to change the boots after a few days if their fit is not correct, provided that you wear them about the house only.

The tongue should be of the soft leather bellows type to ensure a waterproof boot. Be most careful in correctly laying the tongue across your foot in the early days. A badly bunched tongue will cause you much discomfort on a long trek, but once it has acquired this bad set it is almost impossible to change it.

Fastening will usually be by lace and D rings, cleats or a combination of both. The bottom lacings should be reasonably loose, but those up by the neck of the boot should be tight enough to prevent movement of your foot inside the boot, without causing too much constriction.

It is possible to buy foam inner soles from most chemist's shops and these add to your comfort. But their real virtue comes if you carry in your pack a spare pair. After a particularly damp day's walking the dry pair can be inserted to give the impression of an almost dry boot.

On no account venture out on a trek until the new boots become moulded to your feet and properly broken in. Discount weird stories you may hear about achieving this by standing in hot water or even worse. Wear them around the house, and if possible at your work. Then take short walks carrying a loaded pack so that the extra weight spreads the soles of your feet. Only when you can slip them on to walk about in comfort are they ready to take you into the hills.

Treat your boots with care. Give them liberal dressings of dubbin to soften the leather and make them waterproof. Keep dubbin away from the toe cap and stiffener at the back of the boot, which should be treated with ordinary shoe polish. Never attempt to dry off damp boots with heat. Newspaper pushed inside will assist drying but a flow of dry air is the best. Immediately after a trek remove any mud. Drying mud will rapidly dehydrate the leather, with the possibility of cracking. Remove small stones that may have become wedged in the Vibram tread.

After many miles the tread on the moulded sole may become worn, and a good boot will benefit from the fitting of a new sole. Your boot shop will usually arrange this for you so that your original investment will last for many years.

4. Choosing your pack

Probably the most important development in equipment design has been the evolution of the frame and pack method of carrying. Without this it is doubtful if backpacking would have achieved its great popularity. It means that ordinary people of a standard physique can carry for miles loads not considered possible in the old days of hiking.

For years the standard pack was the Bergen rucksack. This consisted of a light wooden triangular frame and a heavy canvas bag, and all the weight was suspended from the shoulders. To counteract this backwards drag, the unfortunate bearer was obliged to lean forward in a way that was uncomfortable and inefficient.

The introduction of the modern frame and sack was an enormous improvement. The frame is usually of welded tubular aluminium and resembles a ladder, curved to fit easily against the bearer's back. The bag, with compartments and pockets, is fastened to this frame by various means. The whole thing probably weighs about 5 pounds (2.3 kilograms) against the probable 7 pounds (3.2 kilograms) of the old Bergen.

But the most important feature has been the change in the design of weight distribution. The modern frame still has shoulder straps, but these are largely to stop the bag falling sideways or backwards. Ninety-five per cent of the weight is carried by a padded belt which fastens like a saddle round the load-bearing pelvis. The whole weight now presses down in a line parallel with the bearer's own gravity line instead of pulling out and down. The days of chafed and aching shoulders and head down pulling against the weight are happily over for the backpacker.

The correct frame

There are many types of frame from which you can make your choice, and these are in a range of sizes to meet the varying lengths of trunk. Be sure you try several to get the most comfortable fit for your particular shape.

Look carefully at the construction. A frame is subject to a lot of abuse. When a fully loaded pack and frame are dropped on to one side support, considerable distortion and weakening of the welded joints can occur. Stand the pack on one of its uprights and press down diagonally at the top of the other and observe how it stands the strain (not too hard, of course, or you could be obliged to buy it).

There will probably be straps across to keep the load away from the bearer's back. Ideally this will be a nylon net for good ventilation, with some method of adjusting as the net grows slack. Shoulder straps should be well padded and possibly tapered, with

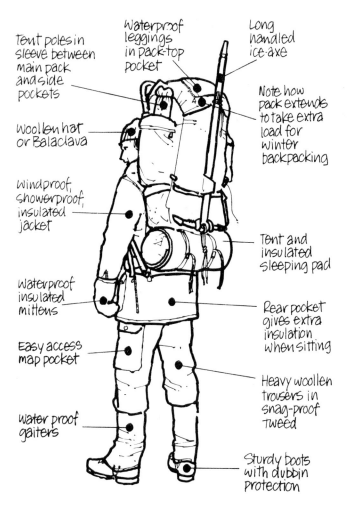

Tent poles in sleeve between main pack and side pockets

Waterproof leggings in pack-top pocket

Long handled ice-axe

Note how pack extends to take extra load for winter backpacking

Woollen hat or Balaclava

Windproof, showerproof, insulated jacket

Tent and insulated sleeping pad

Waterproof insulated mittens

Rear pocket gives extra insulation when sitting

Easy access map pocket

Heavy woollen trousers in snag-proof tweed

Water proof gaiters

Sturdy boots with dubbin protection

Fig. 1. Backpacker with typical winter kit.

16

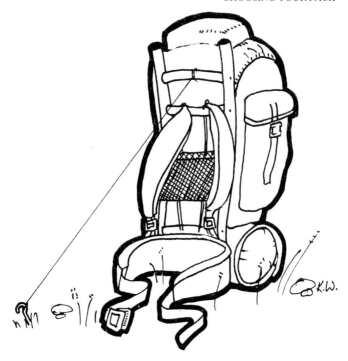

Fig. 2. A simple attachment supports the pack vertically in open country.

quick adjustment buckles. If the feet are not of non-slip plastic then you could fit rubber walking-stick ferrules yourself. Study the hip-belt buckle. It must have a foolproof quick release for there may come a time when you need to discard your pack instantly. A rung at the very top of the frame is useful when lifting, but check that this does not prevent you tipping back your head to look up when you are carrying. A useful device that you can fit yourself is a tent peg on a cord fastened to the top of the frame. This allows the pack to stand unsupported when you are taking a breather.

Bags of all types

You will no doubt find the choice of bags confusing. It is probably best to study them all and decide for yourself which one is most likely to meet your requirements. Here are a few points that you could look for. The material will probably be water-

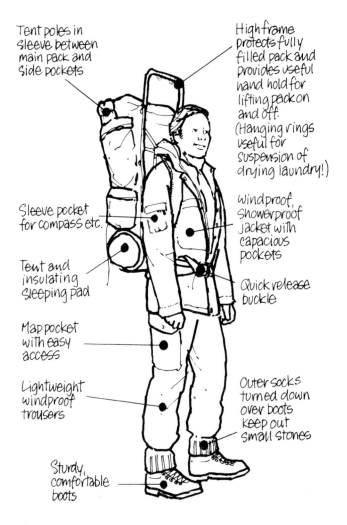

Tent poles in sleeve between main pack and side pockets

High frame protects fully filled pack and provides useful hand hold for lifting pack on and off. (Hanging rings useful for suspension of drying laundry!)

Sleeve pocket for compass etc.

Tent and insulating sleeping pad

Map pocket with easy access

Lightweight windproof trousers

Windproof, showerproof jacket with capacious pockets

Quick release buckle

Outer socks turned down over boots keep out small stones

Sturdy, comfortable boots

Fig. 3. Backpacker with typical summer kit.

18

proofed rip-stop nylon but there are still canvas and cotton bags available. Choose a bag with a large enough capacity for your most ambitious expedition; you are not required to fill it completely when you go off for just two or three days. A bag with top and bottom compartments avoids having to unload everything if the item you require is nestling at the bottom. Side pockets are useful for ensuring that small items are quickly available without a major unpacking operation. Pockets should have robust plastic zips that do not easily freeze, covered by deep rainproof and snowproof flaps. The main bag should have a large flap which gives you great versatility in the size of load you carry. Top fastenings should be of quick-release toggles. Untying frozen cords with equally frozen fingers is unedifying. Some sacks are designed with an all-round zip which allows you to open your pack like a suitcase, but study the strength of the zip. If this fails on a long trek you could be in serious trouble. Small pockets should ideally be tapered to the bottom. It is possible to push in an object the same width as the pocket but when you come to extract it, with no room for your fingers, you can have problems.

A popular carrying combination in recent years has been the frameless pack. This still uses the hip-belt load-bearing principle and sometimes incorporates some kind of frame within the bag itself. Its advantages are still less weight, perhaps more stability and certainly less inconvenience when stowing it in a tent or when boarding a crowded bus. However, there is less room for ventilation at the wearer's back and this may cause discomfort for some.

But these are only points to consider. By the time this book is published a better version will no doubt have been designed and you must evaluate and decide.

Packing your bag

No bag is completely waterproof. Snow and rain can be very insidious and will gain an entry somehow. You may find it helps to apply sealant to the rows of stitching on the seams. Equipment should first be grouped and packed into waterproof bags. These could well be the plastic carrier bags you get from the supermarket although your camping shop will be pleased to sell you specially made, toggle-closing bags. These bags improve the chances of keeping kit dry in the worst conditions and will also simplify packing and unpacking.

Devise a proper place in the pack for everything depending upon its frequency of use. Once you have decided and proved this distribution then strictly adhere to it. Some dark night, in a cramped tent, when you are a little too tired, you are going to be thankful for the discipline that led your hand unerringly to the exact spot in your pack.

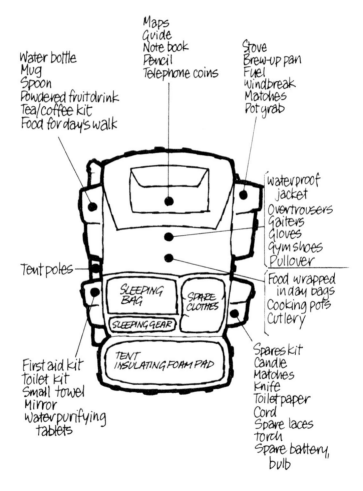

Maps
Guide
Note book
Pencil
Telephone coins

Stove
Brew-up pan
Fuel
Windbreak
Matches
Pot grab

Water bottle
Mug
Spoon
Powdered fruit drink
Tea/coffee kit
Food for day's walk

Waterproof
jacket
Overtrousers
Gaiters
Gloves
Gym shoes
Pullover

Tent poles

Food wrapped
in day bags
Cooking pots
Cutlery

SLEEPING BAG

SPARE CLOTHES

SLEEPING GEAR

TENT
INSULATING FOAM PAD

First aid kit
Toilet kit
Small towel
Mirror
Water purifying
tablets

Spares kit
Candle
Matches
Knife
Toilet paper
Cord
Spare laces
Torch
Spare battery,
bulb

Fig. 4. Suggested location of equipment in typical two compartment sack with side pockets

5. The backpacker's wardrobe

Despite what Eve may have thought, clothes are worn to maintain a body temperature around 98.4 Fahrenheit (36.9 Centigrade).

When air temperature gets too hot, then the body's excess heat must be conducted away. When the air gets cooler then the resulting heat loss must be arrested.

While most people use a whole range of clothes to achieve this control, the backpacker, who carries his wardrobe with him, must assemble a collection of great efficiency. His clothes are best regarded as a heat-control system where various garments, chosen for their different characteristics, are added or removed as necessary.

Heat escapes from the pores of the body as moisture vapour. The first layer of clothing must be able to wick away this vapour, but retain an insulating layer of air. Underclothing of wool or cotton performs this more efficiently than that of man-made fibres. The fishnet type of clothing, with its ability to trap a layer of air, is particularly good. When it was first developed in the Second World War and was issued to parachutists, it was treated as a military secret.

Wonderful wool

On top of this goes another layer able to pass moisture but retain heat. Wool has excellent properties for this purpose. It easily passes moisture, has excellent heat-retaining characteristics and feels warm and pleasant to the skin. This layer usually takes the form of a long shirt and trousers. The shirt should be long enough to cover the whole of the trunk, with full-length front opening and long sleeves. This permits control to be simply achieved when walking by fastening and unfastening the front and rolling sleeves up or down. Whilst your camping shop has excellent versions in bright, attractive colours, your local Marks and Spencer can provide similar garments at a very good price.

Outdoor shops stock special walking trousers or knee-length breeches in various wool mixes and the choice depends upon the backpacker's personal preferences. Jeans are quite unsuitable. The material traps no heat and once wet takes a long time to dry. The budget buyer may well visit the local shop patronised by the agricultural community, who instinctively know about keeping warm. There you can obtain wool-mixture snag-proof trousers, fully cut to give maximum freedom of movement, at a very good price indeed.

Unfortunately wool is neither windproof nor rainproof and in conditions of high wind, which can whip away heat at an alarming rate, a different kind of layer is required.

This is achieved by a shell of tight-weave cotton like poplin or ventile. Ventile was another development of the Second World War when British flyers were demanding lightweight windproof garments. Cotton also has the advantage that, when wet, the threads swell to form a very good barrier against rain. This garment should be lightweight, with large flapped pockets, flap-covered front-opening zip and hood. I have had for years an excellent garment that weighs just 1 pound (454 grams).

The rain barrier of waterproofed nylon

The waterproof qualities of cotton, however, are not good enough in conditions of continuous or driving rain, and a further shell layer is required that is quite watertight. Here the backpacker uses a garment of man-made nylon coated with an impermeable proofing layer. This should be light to carry, with flap-covered front-opening zip and hood. The nylon itself is not waterproof but relies on the proofing layer which is usually polyurethane. Hip belt and shoulder straps unavoidably cause chafing and wear of this layer and so the efficiency of the water barrier is reduced; this must be borne in mind when purchasing and during use. The choice appears to be between buying an expensive garment with several proofing layers or a cheaper garment which is easily replaced. The efficiency of the proofed nylon means that rainwater runs straight off to be deposited very largely on the trousers and if these are not protected the whole exercise seems hardly worthwhile. So waterproof leggings or overtrousers are essential. When selecting these you may like to remember that leggings give better ventilation at the crotch than overtrousers and that the bottoms must be adjustable to allow them to be quickly pulled on over boots.

Unfortunately the complete resistance to water of proofed nylon works both ways, and the process of body-vapour dissipation is brought to a stop. This collects on the inside of the garment as condensation. After a long period of wear the inside will appear as wet as the outside. For this reason these garments tend to be worn only as long as absolutely necessary.

A new and as yet expensive material called Gore-tex appears to have overcome this problem. Gore-tex is a sandwich material with two outside layers of unproofed nylon. The inner layer is of polytetrafluoroethylene (PTFE) that has undergone a process to give a thin three-dimensional matrix structure with microporous spaces. These spaces are too small to allow through a molecule of water but allow the small molecules of water vapour to pass freely. Thus rain is kept out, and body moisture is allowed to disperse. At the moment there are still difficulties in that body oils carried on the vapour are deposited on the matrix, which in turn reduces the surface tension of the rainwater, allowing it, in some instances, to pass through. For this reason the garment must be cleaned at frequent intervals.

The head is responsible for a very large heat loss and a woollen hat or balaclava helmet provides an instant heat regulator of great efficiency.

Gloves, or better still mitts, will prevent heat loss from hands swinging in heat-stealing winds, and once again wool is ideal. For really wet conditions or in wet snow fur-lined nylon proofed gloves can be useful.

So that is the complete layer and shell control system. Additional woollen garments can be carried for insertion between the first and outside shell layers, depending upon the temperatures likely to be met. For very cold weather a polar suit is very useful. This resembles a two-piece tracksuit in synthetic fibre pile material and it can be worn as the first layer, or anywhere in the layer system. It also makes ideal in-tent or sleeping wear and is useful if nature makes an outside excursion necessary.

Jackets or waistcoats lined with down provide a very efficient form of insulation; they weigh very little and because of the great compressibility of down take only a small space when packed. However, down is expensive. The lower-cost man-made substitutes like Hollofil and Fiberfill give an almost similar performance with the added advantage, unlike down, that their heat insulation is not reduced when wet.

Constant monitoring of the efficiency of your layer system, with continual adjustments being made to meet the changes in exertion or outside temperatures, will keep you comfortable and efficient. If you are excessively sweating or shivering you are doing something wrong.

Master this system of heat and ventilation control and your backpacking season will encompass all weathers and all climates.

6. Tents and pitching

The backpacker's tent is his shelter against wind and rain. It must be light to carry, easy to pitch, large enough to provide a degree of comfort and good enough to withstand the rain and winds likely to be encountered.

The variety is enormous, and choice is a matter of personal preference. In this chapter we will outline some of the basic features and the points to look for. Do not consider buying a tent until you have seen it erected and compared it against at least ten others. Ask the salesman to demonstrate just how it is erected.

You will have to decide whether you will be going solo backpacking or sharing a tent with a partner. A small one-man tent will weigh about 4 pounds (1.8 kilograms). A one-man tent which will give you a little more room and which could be used at a pinch as a two-man tent will weigh about 5 pounds (2.3 kilograms). A real two-man tent will probably weigh about 8 pounds (3.6 kilograms), which can be divided between the two.

We can briefly consider the shapes here, but this is no real substitute for looking at or crawling in and out of erected tents.

Pyramid

This is a very basic design. The army used a similar shape in the Crimean War and the North American Indian also knew it. Support will either be a single pole in the centre or an A pole giving easier access. The main advantage is generous headroom but the disadvantage is often a weight penalty.

Ridge

This is the shape that most people imagine a tent to be, beloved by generations of Boy Scouts. It is a good sound design, with reasonable headroom all along the tent. A bell-shaped extension at one or both ends is preferable for cooking and storage of kit.

Wedge ridge

This is similar to the ridge tent but has one upright pole shorter than the other. It restricts headroom to the highest pole end but offers a considerable weight saving.

Cheese dish

This is similar to the wedge ridge tent but uses two poles at the front and one or two poles at the rear. This gives easier access and good head and shoulder room when sitting at the entrance to cook in bad weather.

Tunnel tent

This type usually has a surprising amount of headroom over the

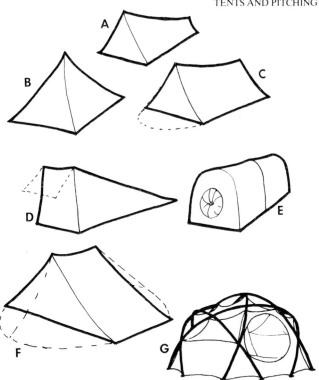

Fig. 5. Basic tent styles. A, Wedge ridge: a combination of the wedge (D) and ridge (C) styles. B, Pyramid: with either central pole or exterior A-shaped frame. C, Ridge: the traditional tent shape, often with bell extension at one or both ends; the two vertical poles may be replaced with external A frames, particularly in a 'mountain' tent; with or without horizontal ridge pole. D, Wedge: two vertical poles, with or without a short horizontal pole, give improved headroom at entrance; often with reversed U-zipped entrance. E, Tunnel: flexible poles, often in sleeves, support this style, which gives good headroom over the whole floor area; often with snow-proof sleeve entrance. F, Truncated ridge: sleepers lie at right angles to ridge, giving wide entrance; often with bell extension to give good storage and cooking area, separate for both. G, Geodesic: when erected this tent is often completely free-standing and may be moved if necessary; it uses flexible poles often housed in sleeves; illustrated is a six-pole version, but simpler versions with three or four poles are available; good headroom over whole floor area.

whole tent area. It often lacks a bell entrance for cooking and kit, and it tends to be heavy.

Truncated ridge

This is a version of the old ridge tent but the ridge is no longer the longest dimension. Advantages are ease of access and the possibility of very spacious bell ends. They are usually two-man tents with an entrance each side. The disadvantage is that the head is under the lowest part of the roof and unless the wall is high this can be unpleasant.

Free standing

A new family of tents makes use of flexible tent poles, stressed to give a free standing structure. Theoretically, if the site is not satisfactory, the tent can be picked up and moved a yard or two. Some claim that it is not even necessary to peg it to the ground, rather relying on the weight of kit and inhabitant to hold it in place. However, one wonders what happens if the occupant is obliged to leave the tent to make adjustments during a high wind. Presumably you chase it down the hill! A very clever version of this is based on the geodesic dome, giving a shape in which most of the interior space is usable.

There are, and will be, many varieties based on these basic shapes.

Lightweight materials

Until the Second World War tents were usually constructed of fine cotton with a waterproof coating, but the most common material now is nylon, with a proofing of polyurethane. This material is completely waterproof, but, as we saw in Chapter 5, this has the disadvantage of not allowing body or cooking vapours to escape. This vapour contacts the cool inner surface of the tent and condenses. The problem has now been overcome by providing an inner tent of nylon which is not polyurethane proofed but silicone proofed. Silicone proofing allows body moisture through, and this then rises to the tent roof, where it condenses. However, when it drops back on to the inner tent roof, the silicone turns it away and it rolls off to the ground. In theory this gives a condensation-free inner tent.

The process is assisted if the doors on the inner tent are always kept open. In the tent you should be dressed to meet the air temperature, and the tent should be considered to be largely a shelter from wind and rain. The difference of between 10 and 20 degrees Fahrenheit (5-11 Centigrade) between a closed inner and an open inner appears to me to be poor compensation for a heavy atmosphere and a condensation-covered sleeping bag.

Choosing a tent

When the tent is erected, check on the separation between inner and outer tents. If this is insufficient a high wind could easily push these together and could break down the silicone proofing. The design of a tent should enable the outer tent to be pitched first. In very foul weather this will then quickly provide shelter for you and your kit. The inner, which will now be kept dry, can be installed when convenient.

The groundsheet should be an integral part of the inner tent. This will be tray-shaped, and the wall height should be checked. Many a backpacker has awoken during a storm to find his tent is sitting in the middle of a two-inch-deep river!

Examine the seams. The double-row stitching should have eight to nine stitches to the inch (25 millimetres). There should be no seam across the groundsheet.

Ideally the pegs should be of the aluminium angle type, but these can be purchased separately for the main guys at least. It is sensible to carry about four spare pegs to replace those that get lost or as an emergency reinforcement when foul weather is expected.

Check that zips are heavy-duty plastic to resist freezing, and that the bottoms of zips have a fastening device to take the strain when the zip is closed. There should also be adequate means of keeping door flaps rolled and fastened when these are open.

If aluminium poles are not corded together, you should code-mark them yourself with different-coloured waterproof adhesive tape. This speeds up erection, especially when you arrive at your pitching place a little weary.

Examine the holes where poles are to be inserted and guyrope attachment points. These should be reinforced sufficiently to take the strains they will surely experience. You will need a separate bag for your poles and another for your tent pegs.

When you finally decide on your tent there is still much to do. You may well consider sealing the seams with one of the many compounds available to prevent water creeping through needle holes. (Some manufacturers solve this by using a cotton-covered man-made thread. When wet, the cotton swells to fill the needle hole.)

Pitching your tent

Practise putting up the tent until you can do it quickly, always achieving a good set. Nylon is best kept tight. The old habit of keeping guy lines slack to allow for shrinkage went out with the departure of cotton. Do not restrict these tent-erecting sessions to the beautiful afternoons when the neighbours are busy putting up their garden shelters. Pick the foul days of wind and driving rain, and practise also in the dark. You will probably get strange looks if this is taking place on your lawn but people can be surprisingly tolerant.

Learning where to pitch will come with experience. In rural areas you will always need the owner's permission. A call at the village shop or, better still, a question over a pint in the village pub will usually provide you with some ideas. Some backpackers aim not to put up their countryside coloured tents until nightfall and then at dawn silently steal away. On the high moors and hills it is a much simpler matter. In Scotland it is easiest of all. You are merely required to avoid cultivated land and shooting seasons.

Watch carefully where you pitch. Avoid charming gulleys which can become streams in a sudden rainstorm. Do not pitch under trees that could drop a dead branch or pine cone on to your tent and which collect the damp of a soft mist until enormous water drops are formed which hammer down on your tent long after the mist has cleared. Study the ground carefully for sharp objects which may pierce your groundsheets or bumps to feel in the night. It is a good idea to lie down and find an acceptable strip and erect the tent on that. If the ground has a slope, try to get your feet lower than your head, but watch always the direction of the wind in relation to the shape of your tent. It is a good idea to take a compass bearing and then check that you will see the sunrise as early as possible. It is very satisfying to watch the dew steaming from your tent while you take breakfast.

Consider the availability of water when you pitch. If it is too far you will have a long walk with your water bucket. If too near you could suffer from damp and insects. When water is taken from a running stream check the map that there is no human habitation just upstream. Boil for three minutes or make liberal use of your water-purifying tablets.

Never wash yourself or your pots in a stream. A little further downstream a backpacker could be filling his water bucket.

When striking your camp, pack the tent so that you know what will come out first. You may next be pitching in the dark. Always count your tent pegs before you move off.

Make it a rule never to have boots in your tent. Cooking pans and stove should be stored between the inner and outer tents. A small square of plastic tucked under the floor of the tent can be slipped out to kneel on when fastening or unfastening the flaps. Never cook in the inner tent. If the weather is bad cook under the awning but otherwise cook outside with a wind shelter for your stove. There is more room and the whole operation is less complicated. Keep your tent tidy and this will lead to less frustration and misplaced kit.

A tent pitched well is a source of great satisfaction and will give you a pride of ownership, especially if it is in one of those delightful spots that you will discover, with views not enjoyed by even the best sited houses in the land.

7. A good night's rest

An experienced backpacker expects to get a good night's sleep anywhere in any conditions – neither too cold, too hot nor too uncomfortable.

A sleeping bag provides a light and convenient form of bedding. The most expensive and the most efficient of these are down-filled. The man-made fibre fillings like Hollofil and Fiberfill are not quite so efficient and do not have quite the same compressibility. However, they have an advantage over down in that their efficiency is not impaired if the filling should get wet.

Manufacturers have introduced many different methods of quilting to ensure the best distribution of the filling with a minimum of cold spots. Zip closures of varying lengths are available but generally the shortest zip means less heat loss. For very cold conditions a bag with a hood is useful as this can help restrict the high rate of heat loss through the head. Various shapes of bags such as tapered bags and barrel-shaped bags aim to meet personal preferences.

Bags are made with various weights of filling to meet various temperature ranges. Manufacturers talk of four-season bags for all-year use, three-season for spring to autumn, two-season for spring and summer and one-season for summer only.

It may seem unnecessary to carry a winter-style bag in the middle of summer but sleeping bags are expensive and most people own one bag, which is usually a compromise. In any case the weight difference between the light two-season models and the heavier winter models is probably only about 1 pound (0.45 kilograms).

Down and the imitation materials obtain their insulation from trapped air caught in the fronds and fibres. If these materials are compressed then this insulation is largely lost. This means that no matter how thick the layer of filler beneath you heat will be lost into cold ground.

Heather for a mattress

For this reason an insulating pad is essential. The most useful are the closed-cell foam mats, which are very light and are generally available in thicknesses of one eighth of an inch (3 millimetres) and three eighths of an inch (10 millimetres). A three eighths of an inch (10 millimetre) mat is usually just large enough to provide a sleeping area and is placed below the sleeping bag in the tent. The one eighth of an inch (3 millimetre size) is often nearer the size of the tent floor area and is inserted beneath the groundsheet when the tent is erected. This assists overall insulation and also helps to protect the groundsheet from damage by small abrasive objects.

Soft turf below the groundsheet provides a good enough mattress. Some people believe in making a depression for the hip but it is my experience that this is only useful for the first few minutes, the hip rarely staying in the hole. Heather and bracken should not be overlooked for providing a most luxurious base. Do not despair if you find sleep difficult on the first few nights. Just accept that you will become very used to it, to the extent that when you return home your bed will feel very strange indeed.

A thin cotton sheet bag can be used inside the sleeping bag to counteract the sometimes cold feel of nylon and also to help keep the sleeping bag clean.

Some backpackers sleep in the underclothes worn during the day but it is usually considered that a complete change should be made for nightwear when possible. A cotton shirt and spare pants will suffice for summer use while a polar suit is ideal for cold conditions.

When possible, the sleeping bag should be aired for a few minutes before packing after a night's use. It is sensible to unpack the sleeping bag about an hour before use to allow it to achieve full expansion and maximum efficiency.

A pillow can usually be made of spare shoes and the bag containing spare clothing.

I usually sleep with both inner and outer tent flaps wide open unless wind and rain suggest that it is imprudent. Even then I close, or partly close, only the outer tent. I prefer to rely on clothing and sleeping bag for warmth.

Pack away all food at night to avoid attracting unwanted visitors. You alone are of very little interest to them. A mosquito net with zip opening, sewn to the inner tent, can be useful at times.

It is a sensible plan always to keep a hand torch in the same place in the tent for instant location in the dark, should the occasion arise.

Before turning in many backpackers prepare the stove and everything required for the first brew-up of the day. There is something very special about waking and drifting into consciousness as the dawn breaks, setting a match to the stove, and snuggling back into the sleeping bag until the singing pot tells you that it is time for tea in bed.

8. Food and cooking

I would have preferred to leave the next few pages blank, with the suggestion that you fill them in after you have acquired some experience, for nowhere is a backpacker's individuality expressed more clearly than in the matter of food. How much, when and what you eat will be decided only by you. But one thing is certain, and that is that you need to eat.

Food is the great provider of energy that will keep your backpacking machine working efficiently and well. It is also a source of warmth, contentment and pleasure

3500 calories a day

With a medium load on your back and walking across friendly terrain you will probably burn up energy at the rate of 3500 calories a day. A strenuous mountain walk in winter could raise this to as much as 5000 a day. If you are to remain fit these calories must be replaced.

Calories come from three main food types: fats, protein and carbohydrates. Fats have about twice as many calories as either protein or carbohydrates, but as digestion takes longer the release of energy is slower. The carbohydrates on the other hand release energy immediately. This means that your reservoir of energy will be looked after mainly by foods with a high fat content while for instant bursts of energy you will look to the carbohydrates like sugar and glucose.

So now you will be looking at food differently from any dieting friends you may have. They are looking for foods of low calorie content, whilst you, because you are going to have to carry it, will be looking for maximum calories with minimum weight.

By using your friends' dieting books it is simple to compose a day's menu that will provide you with 3000 to 4000 calories. However, it is a bigger problem to draw up this menu so that it comes within your acceptable load-carrying limits and is capable of being prepared with your restricted cooking facilities.

But do not let all this worry you. It is just part of the sophistication that you will acquire with experience. Your first expeditions will probably last only two or three days anyway and you will merely take what you think it is sensible to carry. One of my happiest recollections is of a few days that I snatched in the hills when I had only time to stuff chocolate and cheese into my pack and every meal was a trouble-free banquet.

Lightweight foods

It is doubtful if you can get the weight of food you carry down to below 1½ pounds (0.68 kilograms) a day, and you will begin a week's trek with a load of at least 10 pounds (4.5 kilograms). You can see then the importance of carefully drawing up your food lists.

It is best to plan every meal so that you take just enough, rather than trying to estimate quantities you will need to cover the whole period.

Most camping and mountain shops sell specially packed dehydrated and accelerated freeze dried (AFD) foods and these are invaluable in keeping the weight down to acceptable limits. Apart from lightness, many of these have the advantage of a minimum of cooking time, with consequent reduction in the weight of fuel to be carried. However, some of these taste awful, and even the best, after a while, generate a cloying chemical taste in the mouth which becomes unacceptable. They also tend to be expensive. On the other hand, the shelves of your local supermarket present a wealth of light to carry, space-saving, easy to prepare foods.

These include boil-and-serve packet soups, meat extract cubes, instant rice dishes, soya protein preparations, instant mashed potatoes and dehydrated vegetables.

Now you really can become cunning and creative. With a little thought here and a stroke of genius there you can compile a menu that is low in weight, quickly prepared, a joy to consume and a precious memory for ever.

Your nearest delicatessen has a wealth of suitable items and the shelves of your health shop will offer a number of ideas.

Here are a few tips.

Avoid anything in heavy containers. There is also no sense in carrying unnecessary liquid, so avoid anything with a high water content. Learn to do without butter; it always seems to be either frozen into a block or running out of whatever container you use; instead use the excellent tubes of soft cheese, some of which have exciting additions like chives or ham or shrimps. Get the wonderful tubes of Nestles condensed milk, ideal for tea and superb for making an otherwise mediocre sweet dish into a gourmet dish. Some of the instant custard mixes are good and some of the instant omelette mixes make wonderful pancakes. Individual sachet portions of sauce, salad cream and mustard are worth finding space for. A sachet of mixed herbs will enable you to lift the dullest food to extraordinary heights of culinary perfection.

Do not overlook the fact that some fresh foods, especially if you are winter backpacking, will keep for several days. Bacon wrapped in foil provides its own cooking fat, and a small steak is a very acceptable weight penalty. Eggs are good for three days, can be quickly cooked and contain plenty of quickly absorbed protein. (Break them into a plastic wide-topped bottle and you can easily pour them out one at a time.)

It is important that you try out all your meal ideas at home. It is not the time for experiments when you are high on the hill, tired and hungry. Remember also that meals can be very much simpler than you normally eat at home. There is no need to titillate the digestive system by the sight of meat and three vegetables attractively arranged on a white china plate. A thick stew, eaten with a spoon from the cooking pan, provides a feast. The open air gives any meal a certain splendour and Don Quixote wisely said that the best sauce in the world was hunger.

Make up a ration bag for each day of the trek and put in this all the food you have planned for that day. Prepack separately and clearly label each meal. Include all snacks like chocolate and Mars bars to be nibbled en route and your tea-making ingredients. This saves the chaos that can arise from scratching around in an all-purpose supply bag within a cramped, poorly lit tent. It is also a simple way of ensuring that your food lasts out the whole trek.

If your route includes a village it may be possible to supplement your rations by buying enough fresh food for a couple of meals. Ham, sausages and paté are all very acceptable acquisitions. Fresh fruit and milk can also be bought and quickly disposed of.

Several fresh vegetables like carrots, onions, cauliflower and brussels sprouts can be eaten without cooking. And if your proposed night pitch is not far away, you could even buy a small tin of fruit to be smothered by your Nestles milk.

On long treks of two to three weeks it is possible to dispatch food parcels to yourself for collection at post offices en route.

Cooking in camp

The traditional image of camping includes cooking over an open campfire but this rarely happens today. We are much too concerned with the fragility of the environment. Instead the backpacker carries one of the lightweight stoves which have been developed over recent years.

Your local camping shop will show you the various types and you can decide which one you believe best suits your purpose. Basically, these are divided between the butane gas burners and the liquid fuel types.

Probably most popular are the butane gas types. These use small, light gas cylinders, which are obtainable practically everywhere. Cylinders are either self-sealing or non-sealable. The non-sealing cylinder must never be removed from the stove before it is completely empty. The stoves are simple to operate and the heat easily controlled. A disadvantage, especially for the high-level or winter backpacker, is the poor performance in low temperatures.

Petrol and paraffin stoves both work with the fuel under pressure. Petrol stoves tend to be very efficient and the fuel is available everywhere, but a great deal of care is required in their use. Paraffin is perhaps not so demanding but the smell of the fuel does

Fig. 6.   Typical cooking arrangement with methylated spirit stove, plastic water carrier, pot-grab, mug with spoon attached, light weight knife and spoon, meal bag, combined pepper and salt holder. The windshield is made of kitchen foil and bicycle spokes.

very easily permeate the whole of the backpacker's kit, including his food.

After experimenting with every type of stove my preference is for those burning methylated spirit, especially those which incorporate a deep pot-enveloping windshield. I find them to be simple and foolproof. You probably need to carry more liquid than with the pressure fuels types but with careful husbanding of the generated heat they can be most efficient. The fuel is available at most hardware shops and chemists.

A windscreen is sensible for use with all stoves to prevent winds whipping away the heat, although with the integrated-windshield meths burners this problem is largely overcome. An efficient screen is easily made by pushing four bicycle spokes into the ground around the stove and then pressing on to them a sheet of cooking foil.

Lightweight pots and pans come in all sizes, but restrict yourself to two deep pots and one shallow pan which may be used as a frying pan or plate. Both pots should have lids. Avoid any handles on pans. These either get hot and burn unwary fingers or present protuberances that are too easily knocked, to end in an upset meal. It is better to use the simple aluminium pot tongs, which should always be kept in the same spot by the stove for instant removal of a pan from the heat.

The wise backpacker will keep at least three plastic-wrapped matchboxes in different places in his kit to ensure having a supply of dry matches. I usually carry a couple of 9-inch (229 millimetre) diameter plates pressed out of aluminium foil. They are cheap, practically weightless and usually last out a trip. I use them when stacking pans during cooking, as a lid for the frying pan, as a plate, or for providing a working surface during cooking.

You will need to drink plenty of liquid to replace that lost by perspiration and a water bottle is essential. You will probably keep this topped up for brewing tea during the day's walk. This may be a plastic wide-necked bottle which easily fits into one of the outside pockets on your pack. Water purification tablets must be dropped into the bottle whenever water is taken from a doubtful source. For use in camp, a collapsible plastic bucket will probably be most use. The transparent type enables you always to see the water level.

You will need a mug. A plastic type rather than aluminium will mean that you can drink your tea or soup while it is hot, and you

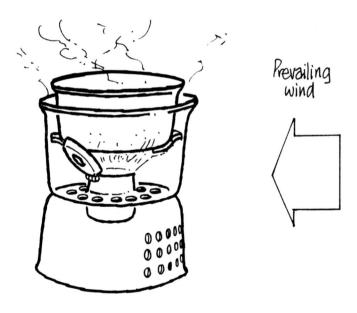

Prevailing wind

Fig. 7. How the methylated spirit stove works.

35

can easily mark it at the ⅓ pint (0.19 litre) and ¼ pint (0.14 litre) levels for use as a measure when reconstituting dehydrated foods.

A knife is essential and so is a spoon. A fork only seems to be useful when prodding frying sausages!

Spare meal

In a trek of several days it is sensible to carry a spare meal in case something goes awry with your calculations or your programme. And finally, deep down in your pack, you should secrete a delicacy to be taken when morale is low or when a celebration is called for. A small aluminium can of sardines, for instance, suddenly remembered, can provide one of the highlights of an expedition.

Ready to go

So now you are equipped and all ready to go on your first backpacking adventure. In the next chapter we consider where.

9. Where to go backpacking

Where do you go backpacking? The answer is anywhere. Stick a pin in a map of Britain or indeed Europe, and as long as you have avoided a city centre you are in potential backpacking country.

The great thing about backpacking is the way it opens up the wilderness areas for exploration and wandering. But to get the experience you need, and to keep you and your techniques in condition, you need only travel to the edge of your town or village. The wilderness begins at the first footpath sign you come to.

A home-ground adventure

So begin with a trial home-ground adventure. The advantages of practising on your home ground are obvious. First of all, you avoid spending valuable time travelling to a starting point, and you commence walking almost straightaway. It probably also means that you will get away more weekends than you would if expensive rail fares or petrol miles had to be considered. But it also means (and we will not dwell on this point) that if you *have* forgotten something, or your new boots are a disaster, or the weather suddenly behaves very unkindly, then you can easily retreat. And you will be a lot wiser and better prepared to fight another day.

You will first need one of the Ordnance Survey's excellent 1 to 50,000 maps covering your area. It will be either a First or a Second Series map, depending on how the Ordnance Survey's revision programme is progressing, but either will do very well. Study the map and plot a route using as many footpaths (small red dots) and bridlepaths (red dashes) as possible. It is estimated that in England and Wales there are about 100,000 miles (160,000 kilometres) of public footpaths to choose from. You will have to connect these with minor roads (brown, yellow or white) and occasionally main roads (red). Find on the map a suitable start point like a village on a bus route or a convenient car park. (A public house car park is ideal, but do ask permission and remember they are there to sell refreshment!) Your route should either take you to another bus stop or bring you back to your car.

Try to find a route which contains some interesting features. There is no need to spend all day walking along hedgerows. Look for a high point which gives you a view over where you have walked or, better still, where you propose to walk. Search for a path by a stream, a waterfall or through a wood.

A map is a picture-book

The Ordnance Survey 1 to 50,000 map is not just a plan of Britain's road system. It contains a wealth of information. Learn to read your map like a picture-book.

It will show you where the path is steep or where it traverses a high ridge or wanders along a valley. It shows streams and footbridges, woods and spinneys, old disused airfields and railways, quarries and earthworks, bracken and heathland. It shows overhead power lines, which are useful in determining your exact position when out on your trek, and it tells you whether the church you should be able to see has a spire or a tower. You are even advised if a windmill (usually a sign of a good viewpoint) is in use or not.

An experienced map user can take any point on a map and fairly accurately describe what he would see in front of him almost as if he were there. Cultivate this skill in rural lowland areas and the chances of you getting lost on the high hills become satisfactorily remote.

Use your compass

A compass is as essential as a good map. It will help keep you on your course where there is no track or where the path divides or becomes indistinct. It will enable you to align your map correctly, and it will show you exactly where you are on that map, when you just need to check your position or when you believe yourself to be completely lost.

It is invaluable to the backpacker, but only if he knows how to use it quickly and correctly. It is no use just carrying it and only looking at it when visibility is down to 15 feet (4.5 metres) on some wild fell and expecting it, in some way, to lead you to safety. Practise using it on clear days when you can see your mistakes and when it does not matter if you make them.

The growth of the sport of orienteering has put some very good compasses in the shops. Best known are those produced by Silva, who also provide a useful leaflet outlining the various ways the compass should be used and with some suggested training exercises.

How far to walk

In planning your route learn to talk not of how many miles, but of how many hours walking.

This again is where close study of the map will keep you from trouble. Along a flat, well defined path or green track you may well cover something like 4 or 5 miles (6.4 to 8 kilometres) an hour, but this will be slowed down by steep ascents and even descents. Progress will be slow in lowland cultivated areas where you may divert round fields and need to climb stiles and open gates. You will probably also spend a great deal of time checking your map, whereas in hilly country you can often see the feature you are aiming for several miles away. If there is an average walking speed, it is probably about 2½ miles (4 kilometres) an hour. A rule of thumb for mountain country, which emphasises the need to consider distance as two-dimensional, is Naismith's formula, which suggests you allow one hour for every 3 miles (4.8 kilometres) measured on a flat map with the addition of half an hour for every 1000 feet (300 metres) climbed. A lesser known rule, but almost as useful, is the author's own party rule. This suggests that you add one minute per hour for every member of the party.

Give yourself time to look

When considering how long you will be walking, remember to allow time for meal stops, rest breaks and time just to look. One of the joys of backpacking is the thrill of discovery you will experience.

You are not out just to stretch your legs. You could well do that on a circular track. You are there to see, hear and smell the wonderful land that exists just off the main roads and motorways. Walk like the gourmet eats, and give yourself time to savour all the subtleties.

So put on your boots and your pack and have your 'home-ground' adventures. In no time at all you will be ready and eager for more ambitious journeys, for the real delights of backpacking are yet to come.

Wider horizons

Now that you have some experience of packing, carrying, route finding and pitching you are ready to be more adventurous and can look towards more rewarding backpacking territories.

The choice is enormous and there is a great deal of information readily available to help you.

National Parks

The Countryside Commission (see Chapter 11) will send you details of the ten National Parks.

These are Brecon Beacons, Dartmoor, Exmoor, Lake District, North Yorkshire Moors, Northumberland, Peak District, Pembrokeshire Coast, Snowdonia and Yorkshire Dales. Two new parks are proposed for the South Downs and Norfolk Broads. A National Park is defined as 'an extensive area of beautiful and relatively wild country where the characteristic landscape beauty is strictly preserved; access and facilities for public open-air enjoyment are amply provided; wildlife and buildings and places of architectural and historic interest are suitably protected, while farming area is effectively maintained.' The land in the Parks is not owned by the state, so rights of access are the same as for the rest of the country, and permission to pitch is still required from landowners or tenants.

Long-distance footpaths

Eight long-distance footpaths cover about 1500 miles (2400 kilometres). These include the well known 270-mile (432-kilometre) Pennine Way, which provides rugged, but sometimes over-crowded walking up the spine of England; the 85-mile (136-kilometre) Ridgeway from Buckinghamshire to Wiltshire, giving easy high-level walking but marred in places by farm vehicle and motorcycle tracks; the 80-mile (128-kilometre) South Downs Way from Eastbourne, East Sussex, moving gradually inland to near Petersfield in Hampshire; the 570-mile (912-kilometre) South-West Peninsula Coast Path, which follows spectacular clifftop paths from Minehead, Somerset, all the way round the peninsula to near Bournemouth in Dorset and includes the beautifully wild coasts of Devon and Cornwall; the other clifftop path, the 170-mile (272-kilometre) Pembrokeshire Coast Path; the historic 168-mile (269-kilometre) Offa's Dyke Path, which for most of its route follows an eighth-century earthwork marking the boundary between England and Wales; the North Downs Way, which provides 140 miles (224 kilometres) of fine walking over chalk downs from Farnham, Surrey, to Dover in Kent; and finally the 93-mile (149-kilometre) Cleveland Way, which combines ridgeway, moorland and coastal walking and almost encompasses the North Yorkshire Moors.

Again you can obtain, free of charge, a great deal of information, useful in the planning stages, from the Countryside Commission. All of the paths are covered by guide books of varying degrees of usefulness, which you will find in your local outdoor activity shops.

Scotland

The mecca for British backpackers, however, is Scotland. This beautiful country contains some of the wildest unspoilt territory in the British Isles, and backpackers have a much greater freedom than in England or Wales. It is possible to walk and pitch an overnight tent virtually anywhere on uncultivated land, and there is no law of trespass except when wilful damage is caused. (Landowners do request that you keep off their land at certain times due to lambing, deer-stalking and grouse-shooting.)

It can be very wild, however, with infrequent supply and access points, and the weather can be harsh. You will need to be properly equipped and well experienced to venture across some of the most beautiful of the highlands. But the rewards are great indeed.

Much information is available free of charge. In particular the Highlands and Islands Board produces some excellent, colourful and informative literature.

Backpacking abroad

A network of long-distance footpaths, which make ideal routes for the backpacker, exists in Europe. France has a spectacular total of 6000 miles (9600 kilometres), and Switzerland has well signposted paths over mountains and down valleys. There is delightful walking in Luxembourg and splendid mountain and forest walking in Germany. One path that is a breathtaking 1300 miles (2080 kilometres) long wanders from the Baltic through Germany, Switzerland and northern Italy to the Mediterranean. Sweden, which has no real restrictions on access anywhere, has some wonderful wilderness walking, including the famous 220-mile (352-kilometre) Kungsleden, or Kings Way. In the United States, as you would suppose, there are footpaths of monumental distances.

But the adventure, contentment and sense of achievement that are the rewards of backpacking are available wherever you walk and wherever you pitch – even if home is only a bus ride away.

10. Prepared for anything

It is fairly easy to arrange equipment and to acquire experience to meet all the expected situations. However, the backpacker must also be aware of the unexpected, and as far as possible prepare himself and his kit accordingly.

A first-aid box is an obvious precaution. A small pouch that can be opened with one hand should be carried at the top of a side pocket on your pack. It should be suitably marked; it may not be you looking for it. Careful selection will keep the weight down to less than 9 ounces (255 grams). By making up your own kit you will ensure that you know exactly what is included and how it should be used. The following list will help you in your compilation.

> Small pair round-nosed scissors
> 1 inch (25 millimetre) roller bandage
> 2 inch (50 millimetre) roller bandage
> 6 inch by 4 inch (150 by 100 millimetres) piece of lint
> 1 yard (1 metre) of adhesive tape
> 2 cotton buds
> 1 sterile wound dressing (small)
> 1 sterile wound dressing (large)
> Compressed cotton wool (about golf-ball size)
> Small tube of antiseptic cream
> Collection of elastic adhesive dressings of various sizes
> 1 piece of padded foam Moleskin 4 inches (100 millimetres)
>   by 2¼ inches (57   millimetres)
> Collection of safety pins

You will know best what medicaments you should have with you but these are suggestions.

> 6 throat lozenges
> 6 mouth infection tablets
> 6 indigestion tablets
> 6 constipation tablets
> Aspirin
> 4 Alka-seltzer
> Tube of insect repellent
> 1 small tube insect bite cream
> Water purification tablets
> 6 salt tablets

Consider how you would make a sling and practise with a suitable piece of equipment such as a small towel, neck scarf or even a spare shirt.

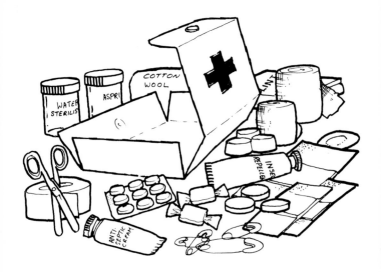

Fig. 8. Typical first-aid box with contents.

Acquire some knowledge of first-aid and be familiar with mouth-to-mouth assisted breathing techniques.

You should bear in mind that in the case of an emergency you should be easily seen from a distance. I have noticed that back-packers whose treks are largely confined to the cultivated country-side sensibly tend to wear browns and greens to blend in with their surroundings, whilst making sure they have some brightly coloured item in their pack. Those who mostly walk in mountains or wilderness areas tend to wear brightly coloured garments. (You will not necessarily have time to extract that piece of bright colour from your pack before you fall off.) It is a matter of preference but should be given some thought.

Always carry a torch with you, not only for seeing what you are doing in the dark but for signalling. Avoid accidental switching on in your pack by reversing the batteries until you are about to use it. Keep a spare bulb and battery fastened to the torch by adhesive tape. A very useful system is the headlamp with waist-belt battery pack as used by potholers. This gives two free hands, with the light beam always in the right place.

You should know how to telephone for help and always have telephone coins immediately to hand.

Before you go into the mountains, know all about the mountain rescue services. Understand how they work, how they can be contacted, and how, if necessary, you can best assist them. And, if you are to be a mountain man, send them a donation once a year. (Consider it as a kind of insurance policy.)

Learn something about weather signs. Get official forecasts whenever possible and then amend continually based upon your own observation of wind, cloud and temperature changes. Know when it is essential that you come down off a hill quickly.

Always carry a whistle. The accepted distress code is six blasts repeated once a minute.

Know the dangers of hypothermia. This is the alarming condition when the body is chilled long enough to lower the body heat core to a temperature at which vital organs cannot perform. It happens very quickly and the conditions that lead to it must be recognised quickly, as must the symptoms themselves. Learn what action to take before and during the critical period. Know too the surprising effects of wind-chill and how normally acceptable temperatures are swept down to killer levels by exposure to strong winds.

The sensible backpacker is aware of sunburn, heat exhaustion and dehydration.

Carry with you some kind of easy-to-nibble emergency rations. Have in your spares kit a candle and windproof matches. If you carry a shaving mirror learn how to use it to signal by the sun. I once did this to good effect over 4 miles (6.4 kilometres) in the Himalayas.

If you plan to walk in the mountains when ice and snow are likely to be encountered, then carry an ice-axe. For the backpacker the long-handled, walking-stick style is probably most suitable. Do get someone to show you how to use it and practise on a gentle slope that levels off. If you consider using crampons, then practise walking in them first, or you will have trouble.

In the mountains carry, and know how to use, a survival bag.

Backpacking is a great adventure. Preparing for the expected will ensure great pleasures, wonderful experiences and lifelong memories. Preparing for the unexpected is a small price to pay.

Off you go

And finally, after collecting together your equipment, deciding upon a route, and actually getting on a track to somewhere, if you meet an ancient backpacker who greets you with a smile and a grunt, please grunt back – it might be me.

11. Organisations and addresses

The Backpackers Club

This organisation surprisingly manages to cater for people who usually consider themselves unorganisable. All members are backpackers. Some are eager novices still planning their first venture. Some are seasoned campaigners. But all are eager to pass on or swap information or knowledge.

The club has a journal called *Backchat*, and this is distributed free to members. Every weekend throughout the backpackers' main season of September to May there is some activity somewhere. Often it is just a few people meeting in a good walking area, with the opportunity to study other people's kit and how they use it.

Training weekends are held throughout the year on a range of subjects such as map reading, navigation, first-aid, lightweight cooking and weather forecasting.

Application forms and membership details are available from: The National Organising Secretary, Eric R. Gurney, 20 St Michaels Road, Tilehurst, Reading, Berkshire, RG3 4RP. Telephone: Reading (0734) 28754.

Other useful addresses

Ramblers Association, 1-4 Crawford Mews, London W1H 1PT.

The Countryside Commission, John Gower House, Crescent Place, Cheltenham, Gloucestershire, GL50 3RA.

Countryside Commission for Scotland, Battleby, Redgorton, Perth, PH1 3EW.

Youth Hostels Association, Trevelyan House, 8 St Stephens Hill, St Albans, Hertfordshire.

The Long Distance Walkers Association, 11 Thorn Bank, Onslow Village, Guildford, Surrey.

The Pennine Way Association, Mr D. Allison, c/o Engineers and Surveyors Department, Council Offices, Littleborough, Lancashire.

The South West Way Association, Kynance, 15 Old Newton Road, Kingskerswell, Newton Abbot, Devon.

Forestry Commission, 25 Savile Row, London W1.

Mountain Rescue Committee, 9 Milldale Avenue, Temple Meads, Buxton, Derbyshire, SK17 9BE.

National Trust, 42 Queen Anne's Gate, London SW1.

National Trust for Scotland, 5 Charlotte Square, Edinburgh, EH2 4DU.

The Society for Sussex Downsmen, 93 Church Road, Hove, East Sussex.

The Offa's Dyke Association, West Street, Knighton, Powys.

The Lyke Wake Walk Club, Cleveland Way Secretary, Potto Hill, Swainby, Northallerton, North Yorkshire.

Central Council for Physical Recreation, 26 Park Crescent, London W1.

Mountaineering Association, 102a Westbourne Grove, London W2.

Mountain Bothies Association, Richard Butrym, Membership Secretary, 15 Merton Road, Histon, Cambridge.

British Mountaineering Council, Crawford House, Precinct Centre, Manchester University, Booth Street East, Manchester.

Camping Club of Great Britain and Ireland Ltd, 11 Lower Grosvenor Place, London SW1W 0EY.

Council for the Protection of Rural England, 4 Hobart Place, London SW1W 0HY.

12. Further reading

Allen, David J. and Imrie, Patrick R. *Discovering the North Downs Way*. Shire Publications.

Bell, Mervyn. *Britain's National Parks*. David and Charles.

Burden, Vera. *Discovering the Ridgeway*. Shire Publications.

Darlington, Arnold. *The Natural History of Britain, Mountains and Moorlands*. Hodder and Stoughton.

Dyer, James. *Discovering Archaeology in England and Wales*. Shire Publications.

Jackson, John. *Safety on Mountains*. British Mountaineering Council.

Lamb, Cadbury. *Inn Signs*. Shire Publications.

Millar, T.G. *Long Distance Paths of England and Wales*. David and Charles.

Peel, J.H.B. *Along the Green Roads of Britain*. Cassell.

Renouf, Jane and Hulse, Stewart. *First Aid for Hill Walkers*. Penguin.

Taylor, Christopher. *Roads and Tracks of Britain*. Dent.

Unwin, David J. *Mountain Weather for Climbers*. Cordee.

Wainwright, Richard. *A Guide to the Prehistoric Remains in Britain*. Constable.

Westacott, H.D. *Discovering Walking*. Shire Publications.

Index